The ***Cuisinart Griddler*** Cookbook

"Delicious and healthy meals for those of us on the go."

Sarah Swanson

Why Use the Cuisinart Griddler

Not just a griddler. It's a full grill, a panini press, quesadilla maker, a life-saver!

So you're the proud new owner of a Cuisinart Griddler. Seriously, it's not just a griddler. It's the most versatile machine in your kitchen and it promises to make your life easier. This book will help you keep using your griddler so that you never run out of delicious ideas to make. Think its just for sandwiches and eggs?

Think again! This fantastic machine has way more sneaky uses than you realized. With very little planning, you can throw a complete meal together in little time!

So what can the Cuisinart Griddler do for you?
- **Cleanup is a dream** -- remove plates & rinse with soap and water! Clean the drip tray. Done
- **Cooks meat fast...really fast** -- seriously, do NOT walk away!
- **Grill inside** when the weather outside sucks!
- **Avoid nasty grease splatters** with our guide on choosing the right meats
- **Save time** making filling meals quickly

Ok, you probably don't care about all the specifics of this grill. Let's get onto to the good eating!

Who this book is for

This book is for the student who is late for class and still didn't eat breakfast.

This book is for the busy mom who has to feed her kids and husband AND still get ready for a full day.

This book is for anyone who is constantly "on the go".

No more making excuses for eating unhealthy crap because we're "too busy."

What not to use this griddler for

Let's face it. There are some things that this grill just wasn't designed to make. There are always sneaky tactics we can take....but some things are just best left alone.

For example, this machine just won't do justice to thick-cut meats like steak. Why would you want to ruin such a fine piece of meat anyway?

That doesn't mean that you can never cook steak in it. Hell, that's probably why most of you even purchased this grill. Some people have reported that really thick cuts of meat tend to cook unevenly, so use this knowledge to your advantage!

The trick is to beat down these cuts with a wooden mallet to allow heat to transfer through the thick meat easier.

And you should also avoid fatty meats while you're at it. Many people have complained that the grease tray doesn't do a good job containing the oily sludge. But most of these problems can be solved by using leaner cuts of meat as well as tenderly beating down the thick cuts into thinner pieces.

How to prevent the griddler coating from peeling…

Yes, this is a problem that some people have reported. You don't want to get these tiny shavings in your food, so the best way to avoid this issue is to avoid using forks and knives to scrape the surface of the metal plates.

The best way to clean it is to use scrub pads that won't scratch or damage the coating on the surface. Scrubbers designed to clean glassware, like the *"Scotch Brite No Scratch Scrub Pad"* (the blue one) are ideal for cleaning.

Commonly Used Ingredients

Ultimate Meats
1. Lemongrass Chicken
2. Cilantro Chicken with Lime
3. Grilled Tandoori Chicken
4. Chilli Lime Chicken Burgers
5. Red Wine-Glazed Pepper Steak
6. Spicy Garlic Basil Turkey Sausages
7. Homemade Chicken Tenders

Ultimate Breakfasts
8. Bacon-Stuffed Pancake Surprise
9. The Ultimate Breakfast Griddle
10. Ridiculously Simple Hash Browns
11. Triple Attack Breakfast Monster
12. Fully-Loaded Spanish Omelette

Ultimate Crispy Paninis
13. The Sonny Falconi
14. Ultimate Grilled Cheese
15. Garlic Chicken Panini
16. The Not-Such a Jerk Chicken Panini
17. The Chili Verde Steak Melty
18. Classic Turkey, Bacon and Swiss
19. Roasted Turkey Jalapeño Melty

Ultimate Quesadillas
20. Traditional Chipotle Chicken
21. Picante Spinach Quesadilla
22. Cheesy Broccoli Red Onion Quesadilla
23. Twisted Pepperoni Pizza Quesadilla
24. Steak and Caramelized Onion Quesadilla

Ultimate Desserts
25. Warm Nutella Banana Sandwich
26. Caramel Apple Cream Cheese Quesadilla
27. Easy Pillsbury Cinnabon Rolls
28. Crunchy Peanut Butter & Jelly Sandwich

Quick Meals to Beat Down Your Hunger
29. Grilled Okra and Tomatoes
30. Smashed Potatoes with Gorgonzola and Sage
31. Mixed Corn Succotash
32. Lemon-Glazed Pasta with Veggies
33. Garlic-mint Peas
34. Broccoli with Lemon Crumbs
35. Hearty Red Bell Pepper and Green Bean Toss
36. Creamed Corn
37. Honey-Glazed Carrot Circles
38. Perfectly Roasted Sweet Potato Wedges

Commonly Used Ingredients

Toppings:
Jar of roasted red peppers
Garlic mayo or your favorite spread
Butter
Shredded cheese
Your favorite cheese slices

Bread:
Ciabatta Rolls
French Bread

Meats:
Eggs
Bacon
Sausage
Turkey slices
Chicken breasts
Your favorite deli-sliced meats

Veggies and fruits:
Tomatoes
Onions
Green peppers
Ginger
Potatoes
Garlic
Avocado
Limes
Lemons

Ultimate Meals

1. Lemongrass Chicken

This dish will be a huge favorite to serve up during parties, but it also makes a great appetizer to share on a date. It is perfectly light in flavor -- not too spicy, not too sweet -- just right. Serve it up on skewers and garnish with cilantro to give it a more elegant look.

Ingredients
- 2 stalks lemongrass, peeled and chopped
- 1 shallot, finely diced
- 1 clove garlic, chopped
- 1 teaspoon ginger, grated
- 1 birds eye chili, seeded and chopped
- 1 tablespoon sugar
- 1/2 tablespoon oyster sauce (or soy sauce)
- 1 tablespoon fish sauce
- 1 tablespoon oil
- 1 pound chicken breast, cut into 3/4 inch cubes

Directions:
1. Blend the lemongrass, shallot, garlic, ginger and chili into a fine paste.
2. Mix in the sugar, oyster sauce, fish sauce and oil into the lemongrass paste
3. Marinate the chicken for at least an hour, covered in the fridge. (The longer, the better)
4. Preheat the grill to medium-high heat and slide skewers into the chicken.
5. Close the lid until golden brown on both sides, about 3-5 minutes.

2. Cilantro Chicken with Lime

So you want a healthy alternative to greasy fatty meats? There's something about cilantro chicken that brings the whole family together. With just a dash of lime, this dish promises to curb your hunger with a one-two protein-packed punch. And its delicious!

Ingredients:

- 2 pounds boneless, skinless chicken thighs
- 2 limes
- ½ cup fresh cilantro
- 6 cloves garlic
- 1 tablespoon honey
- 1 tablespoon olive oil
- ¼ to ½ teaspoon salt and pepper
- 1 teaspoon ground coriander

Directions:

1. Drop the chicken thighs in a large bowl or Ziploc bag.
2. Zest the limes over the chicken
3. Squeeze the lime juice into the chicken.
4. Now throw in the cilantro, garlic, honey, olive oil, salt and pepper. Be sure to completely cover the meat.
5. Let the chicken marinate for about 30 minutes at room temperature, or in the fridge overnight. Let the chicken thaw to room temperature before cooking.
6. Preheat broiler or grill. Once its ready, set the thighs on the rack and sprinkle with coriander. Cook 5–6 minutes per side.

3. Grilled Tandoori Chicken

The name tandoori chicken comes from the name of the clay oven the dish is supposed to be prepared in. But if you don't have a giant tandoor oven available at home, the Cuisinart grill is a perfect alternative. The longer you let the chicken marinate, the tastier this dish will turn out -- seriously.

Ingredients:
- 1/2 cup plain yogurt
- 1/2 lemon (juice)
- 1/2 small onion (grated)
- 1 tablespoon garlic (grated)
- 1 tablespoon ginger (grated)
- 1 tablespoon garam masala
- 1 tablespoon paprika
- 1 teaspoon cumin (toasted and ground)
- 1 teaspoon coriander (toasted and ground)
- 1/2 teaspoon cayenne pepper
- salt to taste
- 1 pound chicken (boneless and skinless, cut into 1 inch pieces)

Directions:

1. Mix all the ingredients, but the meat, into a bowl.
2. Drop the chicken in a freezer bag along with the marinade and shake well.
3. Marinate in the fridge for at least an hour, preferably several hours to overnight.
4. Pull the freezer bag out of the fridge and let it sit in room temperature.
5. Remove the chicken from the marinade and skewer it.
6. Preheat the grill.
7. Grill the chicken until cooked, about 3-5 minutes per side.

4. Chili Lime Chicken Burgers

Chicken in any form is a favorite, but with chilli lime? Hallelujah! Prepared with these instructions, your chicken should come out moist and tender and ready to enjoy with healthy, vitamin-dense vegetables such as roasted asparagus, steamed spinach, or sauteed zucchini and butternut squash.

Ingredients:

- 1lb ground chicken
- 2 green onions, chopped
- 1/4 cup chopped red bell pepper
- 2 Tablespoons chopped cilantro
- 2 teaspoons minced garlic
- 1/2 teaspoon salt
- 1/4 teaspoon red pepper flakes
- 1 lime, cut in half
- 4 slices pepper jack cheese
- 4 buns, toasted

For the guacamole:

- 1 avocado
- garlic powder
- salt & pepper
- diced onions
- diced tomatoes

Directions:

To prepare the burgers:

1. Throw in the chicken, green onions, bell pepper, cilantro, garlic, salt, red pepper flakes and lime juice in a large bowl. Mix thoroughly.
2. Form the mixture into 4 even patties and spray each side generously with non-stick spray.
3. Preheat the grill to medium-high. Grill the patties for 3-4 minutes a side, or until cooked all the way through.
4. At the very end, place a slice of cheese on top of each burger, then cover with a large pot lid, and allow to melt for about a minute.
5. Remove burgers to a plate and allow to cool for 5 minutes. Toss it on a toasted bun with your favorite burger toppings.

For the guacamole:

1. Mash all ingredients together with a potato masher or fork.

5. Red Wine Pepper-Glazed Steak

You will pat yourself on the back after pulling this dish off completely in the comfort of your home. Your friends won't believe you made this yourself. You can drink the remaining red wine to reward yourself. Yeah, its that classy.

Ingredients:

- 1 cup red wine
- 1 tbsp black peppercorns
- 1 tsp McCormick Grill Mates Montreal Steak seasoning (or your favorite)
- Pinch of white sugar
- Pinch of salt
- Dash or two of coarse black pepper

Directions:

1. Get out a large saucepan and mix in red wine, peppercorns, Grill Mates seasoning, sugar, salt, and pepper.
2. Let the mixture warm up over medium heat for about 5 minutes, stirring well.
3. Let the sauce cool down and then pour into a big resealable plastic bag.
4. Throw in the steak, seal the bag, and shake vigorously. Refrigerate for at least 1 hour to marinate.
5. Heat the griddler's full grill plates to medium-high. Grill the steak for about 5-8 min if you desire it done medium-rare. Time will depend on thickness of steak, and how you like them cooked.
6. Open the griddler and remove the steaks from the grill. Let them cool for a few minutes to let the sauce absorb into the meat.

6. Spicy Garlic Basil Turkey Sausage

Voila! Another healthy alternative to your favorite unhealthy meaty foods. These turkey sausages can be prepared in less than 10 minutes, then frozen or cooked right away. If you find that you're running in and out the door during workdays, keep a stash of cooked sausages in the freezer. They make a tasty lunch or afternoon snack.

Ingredients:

- 1.3 pounds ground turkey (a 20-ounce package is fine as well)
- 1 tablespoon chopped fresh basil or 1 teaspoon dried basil
- 1 teaspoon crushed garlic
- 1 teaspoon fine sea salt
- 1 teaspoon sweet paprika
- 1/4 teaspoon black pepper
- 1/8 to 1/4 teaspoon cayenne pepper, the more the spicier

Directions:

1. Preheat the grill medium-high heat.
2. In a large mixing bowl, combine the turkey, garlic, paprika, basil, salt, pepper, and cayenne.
3. Using your hands, create 8 equal-sized patties.
4. Spoon a little butter or oil onto the grill plates and set the patties. (If you want to make all 8, use the full grill -- but flip them after 5-6 min)
5. Alternatively, close the lid and grill for 4-5 min, or until browned.

7. Homemade Chicken Tenders

Juicy and crispy chicken tenders just like mom used to make. If you have kids, these will be gone fast, so make sure you get to try one first. Tenders are now easier than ever to make with an indoor grill. You won't ever miss the greasy fast food version anymore.

Ingredients:

- 1 lb chicken breast tenderloins (or use regular chicken breast cut to size)
- 1/2 cup Italian salad dressing
- Juice of 1 lime
- 2 teaspoons of honey

Directions:

1. Pound the chicken breasts to reduce thickness
2. Cut the chicken breasts into medium-sized strips
3. Grab a ziploc bag and throw in the lime juice, honey, salad dressing and chicken strips.
4. Marinate overnight for the best tasting tenders, but at least for 2 hours (unless you're out of time)
5. Preheat your grill on the high heat setting for 4-5 minutes.
6. Set the tenders on the grill plate and space them apart before closing the lid.
7. Grill them for about 4-5 minutes. Be sure to check that they're fully cooked by cutting one in half (it should be white inside)

Ultimate Breakfasts

8. Bacon-Stuffed Pancake Surprise

Who would have thought you could wake up to such a powerful breakfast in the morning? These pancakes are perfect on the weekends. Just the tantalizing aroma of bacon, pancakes and syrup will have the whole family jumping out of bed and to the dining table. The surprise is all in the bacon, in case you didn't get that yet.

Ingredients:

(2 servings)

- 6 slices of bacon
- 1 cup prepared pancake batter (from a mix or <u>from scratch</u>)
- softened butter
- maple syrup

Preparation:

1. Preheat the griddler to medium-high.
2. Throw the bacon on until it's crisp. Remove and place on paper towel.
3. Wipe the griddle gently with paper towels to remove the grease. Leave a little on to let the pancakes cook.
4. Throw the bacon back on the grill, but spaced apart an inch or two.
5. Slowly pour the batter over the bacon strips.
6. Flip the pancake when browned and remove once both sides are done.

9. The Ultimate Breakfast Griddle

Are you tired of feeling sluggish at work? Put that energy shot down and feed your body a nutritious breakfast instead. You can make a tasty protein-packed griddle that will give you the boost of energy you crave in the mornings. Opt for fresher and higher-quality ingredients to increase the energy surge.

Ingredients:

    4 frozen whole wheat waffles, toasted
    3-4 eggs
    Salt and pepper, to taste
    1 Tablespoon butter
    2 cooked sausage patties

Instructions:

1. Preheat the grill to medium.
2. Crack the eggs into a beaker. Add butter, salt, and pepper.
3. Scramble the mixture and pour the eggs onto the grill.
4. Crumble the sausage patties into the eggs or let them cook as patties if you prefer.
5. Add cheese as the eggs are just about done cooking.
6. Assemble sandwiches and top with butter and syrup. To make these for "on-the-go", spread a little butter and jelly inside the waffles before putting the sandwich together.

10. Ridiculously Simple Hash Browns

If you're like most people, you crave crispy hash browns as a side with your eggs and sausage in the morning. Keep a zip loc bag with grated potatoes stashed in the fridge to quickly throw them in the grill in the morning.

Ingredients:

    2 medium russet potatoes, peeled
    1 tablespoon butter, melted
    Salt and ground black pepper, to taste
    Start with a cold panini press or countertop grill.

Directions:

1. Start with a cold grill.
2. Grate the potatoes directly onto the grill plates in 4 big piles. Gently shape the mounds into flat "patties".
3. Drizzle each mound with a bit of the butter, then sprinkle with salt and pepper.
4. Close the grilll and turn on. Cook until crispy and browned, about 6 to 7 minutes. Serve hot and fresh.

11. Triple Attack Breakfast Monster

Meat. Eggs. Cheese. Waffles and syrup. What more do you need to know? Satisfy all the sensations from meaty to sweet and please your palate before rushing off to work. Obviously, the fresher ingredients you use, the healthier and tastier this monster will be. But you already knew that, you smarty-pants.

Ingredients:
½ lb Sausage
½ Cup shredded cheese
1 Egg
Waffles (homemade or frozen)
Syrup (optional)

Directions:

1. Preheat the grill to medium.
2. Pop the waffles in toaster (or make homemade ones)
3. Pour the shredded cheese over the meat in a bowl and mix well.
4. Roll the sausage into a large ball.
5. Flatten into a nice thick patty.
6. Make a hole in the center of the patty with a small cup or bowl
7. Let the meat brown evenly and then crack an egg into the hole in the center. The sausage should be just about done as you let the egg cook.
8. Make sure both sides are cooking evenly.
9. Take that bad boy and throw him between two hot-and-ready waffles.

12. Fully-Loaded Spanish Omelette

Loaded with protein and lacking in all those carbs, you're sure to enjoy this tasty omelette. The protein will keep you going for hours.

Ingredients:
2 slices bacon
1 -ounce fresh spinach
2 eggs
½ cup chopped onions
½ cup diced tomatoes

Directions:
1. Preheat the grill to medium.
2. Set the bacon strips over the grill plates.
3. Cook the bacon until crispy and brown (2-3 min).
4. Remove the bacon, but leave the fat.
5. Throw in the spinach, onions and tomatoes.
6. Pour the eggs over the spinach and close the lid.
7. After 1-2 min (or more depending on how many eggs you use), remove the omelette from the grill.
8. Roll into a cigar or cut into strips to serve with the bacon on the side.

Ultimate Crispy Paninis

13. The Sonny Falconi

Yes, it sounds like an Italian mobster. But you have nothing to fear! This harmless panini is not only delicious, but strangely tantalizing. Put out a hit on your hunger and show your stomach who's boss. Bon appetit!

Ingredients:

- 2 tablespoons unsalted butter
- 3 medium red onions, halved and sliced thinly
- Salt and pepper
- 4 fully-cooked chicken-apple sausage links (such as Aidell's)
- 8 ounces Fontina cheese, shredded
- Garlic mayo
- 1 ciabatta roll, divided into 4 sections, or 4 small ciabatta rolls

Directions:

1. Preheat the grill to medium.
2. Melt the butter in a large skillet over medium heat. Caramelize the onions and season with salt and pepper for 10-15 min, stirring occasionally.
3. Slice the chicken-apple sausage link in half on its longest side but don't cut all the way through.
4. Place the open side of the sausage on the grill and close the lid.
5. Grill the sausages for 4 to 5 min until they are heated through and grill marks appear.
6. Take two ciabatta rolls and sprinkle cheese over one half and spread the garlic mayo over the other.
7. Now add the grilled sausage and caramelized onions and close the sandwich.
8. Press down the lid and grill the panini until the cheese is melted and the bread is toasted, about 4 to 5 min. *Cut in half and serve immediately.*

14. The Ultimate Grilled Cheese

Oh my! This is the meltiest and cheesiest sandwich you will ever try. Grilled to perfection -- crunchy on the outside, chewy and soft on the inside. Caution: you might have to slap some hands away.

Ingredients:

- 2 pieces of french bread
- 1 teaspoon of butter
- 1/4 teaspoon of salt
- 2-3 tablespoons of Mayo
- 1 tablespoon of garlic mayo
- 3 slices of Sharp Cheddar, Colby-Jack and Fontina – one of each (or mix your favorite cheeses)
- 2 Slices of fresh tomato

Directions:

1. Preheat the grill to medium.
2. Butter each slice of french bread
3. Spread the garlic mayo on the bread.
4. Place the three slices of cheese and tomato slices in between the bread halves.
5. Set the sandwich in the grill and close the lid.
6. Cook for 2-3 minutes or until the sandwich is lightly toasted and the cheese is melty. *Serve with fresh fruit for a nice twist.*

15. Garlic Chicken Panini

There's something about the aroma of garlic and spices that lights up a regular panini. You will not regret making this panin. In fact, you might end up making another one.

Ingredients:

- 1 quart water
- 1/4 cup kosher salt
- 2 tablespoons honey
- 1 bay leaf
- 1 crushed garlic clove
- 6 whole black peppercorns
- A dash of dried thyme
- A dash of dried parsley
- Juice of 1/2 lemon
- 1 lb. boneless, skinless chicken breast cutlets (thin-sliced)
- 1 baguette, cut into 4 pieces, halved lengthwise
- Basil garlic mayo
- 1 small jar of marinated artichoke hearts, sliced about 1/4" thick
- 1 small jar of roasted red peppers
- 4 slices Swiss cheese

Directions:

Preparing the chicken:
1. Mix the water, honey, salt, garlic, thyme, lemon juice, and parsley into a large bowl.
2. Now throw in the chicken.
3. Cover the bowl and refrigerate for 30-40 minutes.

Cooking the chicken:
1. Preheat the grill to medium-high heat.
2. Grill the marinated chicken breasts for 3-4 minutes until they're cooked thoroughly.
3. Remove the chicken and turn off the grill to wipe it clean.

To make the sandwich:
1. Preheat the grill to medium heat once again
2. Spread a dollop of garlic mayo inside two baguette halves.
3. Place a chicken breast cutlet on the bottom bread half.
4. Arrange layers of artichoke hearts and roasted red peppers over the chicken.
5. Add a slice of cheese and close the sandwich with the top bread half.
6. Press down the lid and grill the sandwich for 4-5 minutes until the cheese is melted and the bread is toasted.

16. The Not-Such a Jerk Chicken Panini

This version of the classic Jamaican Jerk Chicken is not such a jerk after all. Who gave it such a mean name anyway? You're going to need a lot more ingredients to prepare this awesome panini, but it's absolutely worth it to experience the dance of all the different flavors in your mouth.

Ingredients:

- 1/4 cup malt vinegar (or white vinegar)
- 1 tablespoon dark rum
- 1 jalapeno
- 1/2 red onion, chopped
- 2 green onion tops, chopped
- 1 1/2 teaspoons dried thyme or 1 tablespoon fresh thyme leaves, chopped
- 1 tablespoon olive oil
- 1 teaspoon salt
- 1 teaspoon freshly ground black pepper
- 2 teaspoons ground allspice
- 2 teaspoons ground cinnamon
- 2 teaspoons ground nutmeg
- 2 teaspoons ground ginger
- 1 teaspoon molasses
- 4 boneless, skinless chicken breast cutlets (or 2 chicken breasts cut in half lengthwise)
- 1/4 cup lime juice
- Vegetable oil, for brushing grill grates

Directions:

Marinating the chicken
1. Blend the following ingredients: rum, vinegar, olive oil, onion, hot peppers, onion, green onion tops, thyme, salt, pepper, allspice, nutmeg, ginger, cinnamon, and molasses into a blender. The consistency should be smooth paste.
2. Drop the chicken in a large freezer bag.
3. Add the lime juice and the jerk paste into the bag. Shake vigorously, making sure to coat the chicken thoroughly.
4. Seal the bag and refrigerate overnight.

Making the sandwich
1. Preheat the grill to medium heat.
2. Warm up the pita bread in the microwave on High for about 15-25 sec.
3. Add two slices of cheese in the pita.
4. Add a chicken cutlet and a few spoonfuls of pineapple-black bean salsa and fold the pita.
5. Press down the lid and grill until cheese is nice and melty and grill marks appear (3-4 min).

17. The Chili Verde Steak Melty

Now this panini is the most interesting flavor your mouth will savor all week. It's not overly spicy, but does sizzle your tongue when combined with the steak and cheese. Oh yeah, its a mouthful.

Ingredients:

- 1 pound New York strip steak
- Kosher salt and pepper
- 1 tablespoon extra virgin olive oil
- Chipotle Mayonnaise
- 1 ciabatta loaf or baguette, cut into 4 sections
- 8 slices Monterey Jack cheese
- Caramelized Onions
- 1 7-oz can whole roasted green chiles, chopped

Directions:
1. Generously sprinkle salt and pepper over the steak.
2. Preheat the grill to medium-high heat.
3. Add olive oil after a minute, then the steak.
4. Close the lid and let the steak cook to your preferred doneness. *For medium, cook it until your instant read thermometer reads 137°F.*
5. Remove the steak when its done and set it on a cutting board for 5-10 min.
6. Slice it into thin slices.
7. Cut the bread loaves into two.
8. Spread a tablespoon of mayo inside each half of bread.
9. Add a slice of cheese, the steak, onions, chiles and a second slice of cheese on the top.
10. Close the sandwich with the other slice of bread.
11. Press down the lid and grill the panini until the cheese is nice and melty (4-5 min).

18. The Classic Turkey, Bacon and Swiss

It's all in the name -- turkey, bacon and swiss. With just a few simple ingredients, you can whip up an easy and tasty panini.

Ingredients:
- 4 tablespoons butter
- 8 slices sourdough bread
- 8 slices of turkey breast
- 8 strips of cooked bacon
- 4 slices of Swiss cheese
- garlic basil mayo

Directions:
1. Preheat the grill to medium heat.
2. Spread butter on two slices of bread.
3. Flip over one slice of bread and top it with a few spoonfuls of garlic basil mayo, turkey, bacon and cheese.
4. Close the sandwich with the other slice of bread.
5. Grill two paninis at a time, with the lid closed, until the cheese is melted and the bread is toasted (4-5 min).

19. Roasted Turkey Jalapeño Melty

If you have leftover turkey slices or a nice roasted turkey sitting in the fridge, this is the perfect sandwich to make. Pack it on with more jalapeños to really kick up the spice.

Ingredients:
- 8 slices sourdough bread
- 4 slices Monterey Jack cheese
- Sliced pickled jalapeño peppers
- Leftover roast turkey (sliced or shredded)
- 1-2 tomatoes (thin slices)
- Mayo

Directions:
1. Preheat the grill to medium-high heat.
2. Add a slice of cheese, jalapeños, leftover turkey and tomatoes.
3. Spread a thin layer of mayonnaise on the other slice of bread and close the sandwich.
4. Close the lid and grill until the cheese is melty and the bread is toasted (4-5 min).

Ultimate Quesadillas

20. Traditional Chipotle Chicken

It takes a little longer to prepare, but is worth the trouble. It's sure to tantalize your tongue.

Ingredients:

Chipotle Chicken:
- 3 tablespoons olive oil
- 1 red onion, finely chopped (about 1 1/2 cups)
- Kosher salt and freshly ground black pepper
- 3 garlic cloves, finely chopped
- 5 chipotle chiles in adobo sauce, finely chopped
- 3 vine-ripened tomatoes (about 1 1/4 lbs total), diced
- 3 green onions, thinly sliced
- 1 tablespoon honey
- 3 cups coarsely shredded roasted chicken breast

Quesadillas:
- Four 10-inch-diameter flour tortillas
- 3 cups shredded white cheddar cheese (about 12 ounces)
- 2 avocados, peeled, pitted, sliced
- 1/2 cup fresh cilantro leaves
- 1/3 cup sour cream
- 4 lime wedges

Directions:

Preparing the chipotle chicken:
1. Preheat a skillet to medium-high heat.
2. Spoon some oil in and add the onion, sprinkle with salt, and sauté for about 3 min.
3. Add the garlic and sauté until the onions start to brown (roughly 2 min).
4. Mix in the chipotle chiles and the tomatoes.
5. Cook until most of the liquid from the tomatoes has evaporated and the mixture begins to thicken, stirring often, about 20 minutes.
6. Stir in the green onions and honey slowly.
7. Finally, add the chicken and cook until the chicken is fully cooked.

Making the quesadillas:
1. Preheat the grill to medium-low heat.
2. Place 2 tortillas on the hot grill for about 2 min and then flip them over.
3. Sprinkle 1/2 cup of cheese over the bottom halves of the tortillas and add chicken mixture.
4. Add a little more cheese and top with avocado slices.
5. Fold the tortillas over to cover the fillings and make a crescent shape.
6. Cook until the tortillas are crisp and golden and the cheese has melted (3 min)
7. Sprinkle the cilantro in the quesadilla by opening them just a little. Serve with lime wedges and sour cream.

21. Picante Spinach Quesadillas

Don't be fooled by the name, its not that spicy. Loaded with spinach and cheese, this one is sure to please anyone. It's a sneaky way to load your meals with healthy spinach.

Ingredients:
- 6 oz. baby spinach
- pinch of kosher salt
- 8 small or 4 large tortillas
- 8 oz. pepper jack cheese, grated
- fresh spicy salsa or pico de gallo
- diced or shredded cooked chicken, optional

Directions:
1. Heat ¼ cup of water in a large skillet over medium heat.
2. Throw in the spinach, sprinkle with salt, and cover for about 5 min. Stir well until spinach is soft and tender.
3. Drain the water out thoroughly, until spinach is just almost dry.
4. Preheat the grill to medium-low heat.
5. Place 1-2 tortillas on the warm grill and spread a thin layer of cheese over the surface.
6. Add a layer of spinach leaves evenly over the cheese.
7. When cheese is starting to melt, add a tablespoon of salsa.
8. If desired, add the chipotle chicken mixture over half the tortilla.
9. To seal the quesadilla, fold the side of the tortilla that does not have salsa on it over the top.
10. Close the lid and let it cook for 4-6 min, or until the tortilla is crispy.

22. Cheesy Broccoli Red Onion Quesadilla

You know you should be eating more broccoli, but you're probably not. Tell you what, try this quesadilla and tell me you don't love it. I dare you. Cheese and onions make anything taste great -- even broccoli.

Ingredients:

- 1 large broccoli crown, about 1/2 pound
- 1 tablespoon extra virgin olive oil
- 1 medium red onion, cut in half lengthwise, then sliced across the grain
- 1 tablespoon chopped cilantro or epazote (optional)
- Salt and freshly ground pepper
- 4 corn tortillas
- 2 ounces grated Cheddar or mixed cheeses (1/2 cup)
- Salsa for serving (optional)

Directions:

Making the broccoli filling:
1. Preheat the grill to medium-high heat.
2. Microwave the bag of frozen broccoli as per the instructions on the bag. Or bring a pot of water to a boil and add the broccoli crowns for four minutes and remove.
3. Rinse with cold water and pat them dry with a paper towel.
4. Chop them into small little florets for easier cooking.
5. Spoon some butter over the grill plates and add the red onions.
6. Cook for 4-5 min, or until they start to sear on the edges.
7. Now add the sliced broccoli.
8. Cook, stirring, until broccoli starts to sear as well (roughly 3 min).
9. Remove from the grill and stir in the cilantro, season with salt and pepper.

To make the quesadillas:
1. Drain the water out thoroughly, until spinach is just almost dry.
2. Preheat the grill to medium-low heat.
3. Place 1-2 tortillas on the warm grill and spread a thin layer of cheese over the surface.
4. Add the broccoli filling evenly over the cheese.
5. When cheese is starting to melt, add a tablespoon of salsa.
6. To seal the quesadilla, fold the side of the tortilla that does not have salsa on it over the top.
7. Close the lid and let it cook for 4-6 min, or until the tortilla is crispy.

23. Twisted Pepperoni Pizza Quesadilla

You'll be kicking yourself for not thinking of this yourself. A ridiculously welcome twist on the classic pepperoni pizza. And it's easier to hold and eat so it won't leave your hands feeling greasy.

Ingredients:
- 4 flour tortillas
- 4 ounces of shredded mozzarella cheese
- 3 ounces sliced pepperoni
- 1 (16-ounce) jar of pizza sauce
- butter for pan

Directions:

1. Preheat the grill to medium-high heat.
2. Add a little butter and then the pepperoni until they start becoming crispy (3-4 min).
3. Remove them and place them on a paper towel to drain.
4. Brush each tortilla with a thin layer of pizza sauce.
5. Place the tortilla on the grill and sprinkle cheese on top of the sauce
6. Top with the pepperoni and other toppings, if desired. *Sprinkle with another layer of cheese if you add more toppings.*
7. Close the lid for 4-6 min, or until the tortilla is crispy.
8. Slice into quarters and serve with a little bowl of warm pizza sauce for dipping.

24. Steak and Caramelized Onion Quesadilla

Steak and caramelized onions really do go together well….really well. With a dash of barbecue sauce, this is sure to be a summer favorite to share amongst friends. Plus, its a great way to get rid of all that extra steak.

Ingredients:
- ½ of a steak
- Havarti cheese
- Thyme
- Onions
- Barbecue sauce
- Butter
- 1 tortilla (I used tomato flavoured)
- Garden vegetable cream cheese
- Tomato based pizza/pasta sauce

Directions:

To prepare the steak:
1. Generously sprinkle salt and pepper over the steak.
2. Preheat the grill to medium-high heat.
3. Add olive oil after a minute, then the steak.
4. Close the lid and let the steak cook to your preferred "doneness". For medium, cook it until your meat thermometer reads 137°F.
5. Remove the steak when its done and set it on a cutting board for 5-10 min.
6. Slice it into thin slices.

To make the quesadilla:
1. Preheat the grill to medium heat
2. Add butter and saute the onions for 3-5 min. Remove when done.
3. Melt some butter in your pan until it's sizzling and then place a tortilla on the hot grill.
4. Spread cream cheese on one half and pasta sauce on the other half.
5. Add cheese on one side, then your steak slices, onions, and a pinch of thyme.
6. Close the lid and cook this for about 3-5 min, or until the quesadilla is golden and crispy on both sides. Serve with the barbecue sauce.

Ultimate Desserts

25. Warm Nutella Banana Sandwich

Anybody who says they don't love Nutella is a liar! Now you can use that sweet sweet spread to make a warm and toasty sandwich with mashed bananas. It's surprisingly simple. Once you try warm Nutella on toasted bread, you'll never want to go back. Warning: friends who see you lighting a spoonful of Nutella might give you looks!

Add strawberries to this sandwich to give it an even better twist.

Ingredients:

- 1 ripe banana, sliced
- 4 slices whole-wheat bread
- Nutella spread
- 4 tablespoons unsalted butter, softened
- 1 tablespoon confectioners' sugar (optional)

Directions:

1. Set the bananas in a bowl and mash until they reach a smooth consistency.
2. Spread the Nutella to your liking on 2 slices of bread
3. Now spread the mashed banana over the other 2 slices and combine the slices to make 2 sandwiches.
4. Preheat the grill to medium-low.
5. Spoon a tablespoon of butter over the top and bottom of each sandwich and place on the warm grill.
6. Grill until golden brown (about 3-5 min).
7. Remove from the grill and sprinkle with the confectioners' sugar, if desired. Eat while its hot and fresh.

26. Caramel Apple Cream Cheese Quesadilla

Homemade caramel sauce tastes so much better, but if you must use store-bought, then try to get one that isn't full of chemicals posing as caramel. The cream cheese in this quesadilla goes really well with caramel apples (which are already great on their own).

Ingredients:

Simple Caramel Sauce
- 14 Werther's Original® Baking Caramels, unwrapped
- 1 Tablespoon heavy cream, half-and-half, or full fat milk

Quesadilla
- butter or oil, for the pan
- 4 whole wheat tortillas
- 4-6 ounces cream cheese
- 1 small apple, thinly sliced

Directions:

Preparing the caramel sauce:
1. Grab a small saucepan and add the caramels and heavy cream over low-medium heat. *(You could also use a microwave to melt the caramels and cream together, but you would have to stop and stir every minute or so.)*
2. It is important that you stir constantly and let the caramels melt completely.
3. Once melted, turn off the stove and let the caramel sit in the pan until ready to use.

Making the quesadillas:
1. Preheat the grill to medium-low heat and add butter.
2. Place a tortilla on the grill and top with 1-2 ounces of cream cheese.
3. Top the cream cheese with an even layer of thinly sliced apples.
4. Cover the open tortilla with another one to seal the quesadilla. Press down to make them tight.
5. Close the lid and let the quesadilla cook until the cheese begins to melt (about 3 min).
6. Check on the tortilla every min or so to make sure the bottom is browning.
7. When golden and crispy, remove the quesadilla and place on a large cutting board.
8. Cut into 4 equal pieces and drizzle caramel sauce over the quesadillas. *Serve hot and fresh.*

27. Easy Pillsbury Cinnabon Rolls

This one is a no-brainer. No preparation involved at all! Just pop out a can of Pillsbury Cinnabon rolls and throw them on the grill. They come out toasted and delicious, especially with frosting after they're done.

Ingredients:

- 1 can of Pillsbury Cinnabon Cinnamon Rolls, opened

Directions:

1. Butter both sides of the Cinnabon Cinnamon Rolls and set aside.
2. Preheat the grill to medium-high heat.
3. Place the rolls on the warm grill, giving as much space between each roll as possible.
4. Press the lid down gently to flatten the rolls.
5. Let them cook for 3-4 min, or until browned well.
6. Spread the icing included in the package over them. *Enjoy hot and fresh.*

28. Crunchy Peanut Butter & Jelly Sandwich

Now here's a weird twist on a classic sandwich. Even your 5-year old niece can make a peanut butter jelly sandwich. But can she toast it with crushed cornflakes and make it warm and gooey inside?

Didn't think so.

Ingredients:

- 4 slices of bread
- 1 egg
- A dash of milk
- 1.5 cup cornflakes
- Peanut butter
- Jelly or Jam
- Butter to grease the pan

Directions:

1. Pour cornflakes into bowl and crush them with your hands or a large spoon.
2. Crack an egg with a dash of milk in a separate bowl and beat well.
3. Preheat the grill to medium-low heat.
4. Spread the jelly on one slice of bread and peanut butter on the other slice.
5. Combine them to make a regular peanut butter jelly sandwich.
6. Dip the sandwich in the egg mixture making sure to cover both sides.
7. Now dunk them in the cornflake crumbs.
8. Spoon some butter onto the hot grill and add the sandwich and close the lid.
9. Once the sandwich is golden brown, remove and serve hot and fresh.

Quick Meals to Beat the Hunger

Most of us don't have the time to plan or prepare our meals, or we're just too lazy and make excuses. Whatever your reason for grabbing fast food or eating out excessively, you can easily change the quality of your home-cooked meals by having your ingredients chopped and ready to go in the fridge.

Most of the meals in this cookbook are very filling on their own, but if you're hosting a party or friends come over spontaneously, these ultimate sides are sure to please everyone. And if you're just really hungry….well, mix and match paninis and quesadillas with these sides as you like.

Some of them might require a little preparation outside of the grill, but if you chop and stash ingredients ahead, it won't take very long to get these quick meals ready.

Ultimate Sides

29. Grilled Okra and Tomatoes

No one knows what to do with okra. They're weird and hard to incorporate into many dishes. But as a side? Hallelujah! Now we're talkin'.

Ingredients:

- 1 pound fresh okra, trimmed
- 1 pt. cherry tomatoes
- 2 tablespoons olive oil
- 1/2 teaspoon salt
- 1/2 teaspoon pepper
- 2 tablespoons chopped fresh basil

Directions:

1. Preheat grill to medium-high heat.
2. In a large bowl, combine all the ingredients.
3. Place mixture on cooking grate, and grill, covered with grill lid, over medium-high heat (350° to 400°). Grill tomatoes 3 minutes or just until they begin to pop. Turn okra, and grill, covered with grill lid, 2 to 3 more minutes or until tender.
4. Transfer okra and tomatoes to a serving dish, and sprinkle with basil. *Serve immediately.*

30. Smashed Potatoes with Gorgonzola and Sage

This side does not require using the grill, but is too delicious of a side to leave out. It pairs really well with just about any meat, panini, or quesadilla. If you don't have gorgonzola at home, try it with cheddar for an equally unique flavor.

Ingredients:

- 2 pounds unpeeled Yukon gold potatoes
- 1 1/2 tablespoons butter
- 1/2 cup 1% low-fat milk
- 1/2 teaspoon kosher salt
- 1/2 teaspoon freshly ground black pepper
- 1/4 cup crumbled Gorgonzola or other blue cheese
- 1 tablespoon chopped fresh sage

Directions:

1. Drop the potatoes in a saucepan filled with water (the potatoes should be fully submerged)
2. Bring to a boil for 20 minutes or until the potatoes are tender
3. Drain the water. *Careful, the potatoes will be very hot!*
4. Place the potatoes in a large bowl and mix in butter, milk, salt, and pepper.
5. Mash coarsely with a potato masher (or use the pulse setting in a blender)
6. Add Gorgonzola and chopped fresh sage.

31. Mixed Corn Succotash

This one requires a little preparation outside of the grill…about 2-3 minute's worth. If you're bored of salads with your meat, give this one a shot. You won't regret it.

Ingredients:

- 1 pound fresh fava beans, shelled (1 cup)
- 2 tablespoons olive oil
- 4 cups fresh corn kernels, cut from 4 ears of corn
- 1 small onion, finely diced
- 2 small garlic cloves, minced
- 1 teaspoon kosher salt
- 1/2 red pepper, thinly sliced
- 1 scallion, thinly sliced

Directions:
1. To blanch the fava beans, drop them in a pot of lightly salted boiling water for about 2 minutes
2. Drain and rinse the beans under cold water to stop the cooking.
3. Peel off and discard the green skins; set the beans side.
4. Preheat the grill to medium-high heat.
5. Spoon a little oil on the grill plate and add the corn, onion, garlic, and salt and cook.
6. Using a fork or spoon, stir the vegetables until they are slightly charred and golden (5-7 min).
7. Lastly, add the bell pepper and beans and cook an additional 2 minutes.
8. Remove from heat, add the scallions, and toss well. Serve warm or at room temperature.

32. Lemon-Glazed Veggies with Pasta

Full disclosure: this dish does not use the grill at all. But it's so easy to make and pairs well with chicken and turkey. It doesn't take very long to make either!

Ingredients:

- 1/2 (16-oz.) package rigatoni pasta
- 1 small onion, chopped
- 2 tablespoons olive oil
- 3/4 cup chicken broth
- 2 teaspoons lemon zest
- 2 tablespoons fresh lemon juice
- 1 cup fresh snow peas
- 1 cup matchstick carrots
- 2 tablespoons chopped fresh basil
- 2 tablespoons butter
- 1/2 teaspoon chopped fresh thyme
- 3/4 teaspoon salt
- 1/4 teaspoon freshly ground pepper

Directions:

1. Prepare pasta according to package directions.
2. In a skillet, spoon a little oil or butter over medium-heat.
3. Sauté the onions for 3-5 min, or until slightly browned.
4. Reduce heat to medium and stir in chicken broth, lemon zest, lemon juice, snow peas and carrots.
5. Bring to a boil and cook for 3-4 minutes or until most of the liquid evaporates.
6. Stir in hot cooked pasta, basil, butter, and thyme.
7. Cook, stirring occasionally, for 2-4 min. Season with salt and pepper.

33. Garlic and Mint Peas

This recipe requires some boiling before using the grill. You might have already noticed that the shape of the griddler does not contain water very well. Who would have thought garlic and mint goes really well together?

Ingredients:

- 1 pound sugar snap peas (2 cups)
- 2 cloves garlic, halved
- 1 tablespoon canola oil
- 2 cups fresh or thawed frozen peas
- 1/4 cup fresh mint leaves, chopped, or 1 tablespoon dried mint
- 1/2 teaspoon sugar
- 1/2 teaspoon salt

Directions:

1. Boil a large saucepan of water and add the snap peas for 2-3 minutes.
2. Drain and rinse them under running cold water.
3. Set the griddler to 350 degrees and cook the garlic halves in the oil until golden.
4. Remove and discard the garlic *(unless you finely chopped them, they will be too strong to use with the peas)*
5. Finally, add the sugar snap peas and fresh or thawed peas and cook until tender (3-5 min). *Stirring them with a wooden spoon ensures one side doesn't get burned*
6. Turn off the heat and add the mint, sugar, and salt.

34. Broccoli with Lemon Crumbs

Another quick and tasty way to get more broccoli in your diet. Extra emphasis on the quick and tasty! You can freeze the lemon crumbs for 2-3 days before they start going bad.

Ingredients:

- 2 slices whole-wheat bread
- 2 tablespoons butter
- 1 lemon
- Olive oil
- 1/2 teaspoon kosher salt
- Freshly ground black pepper
- 2 12-ounce bags broccoli florets, or
- 1 large bunch broccoli, cut into florets

Directions:

Making the lemon crumbs:
1. Throw the bread in a food processor or blender to make bread crumbs.
2. Melt the butter in either a small skillet or on the grill.
3. Add the bread crumbs and sauté over medium heat until toasted.
4. Grate the zest from the lemon and cut the lemon in half to squeeze the juice into the pan (half should be enough).
5. Mix in the salt and black pepper and cook, stirring constantly with a wooden spoon, until dry.

Preparing the broccoli:

1. To save extra time, you can cook the broccoli florets right in their microwavable bag. (Or, you can boil them for 4-5 min)
2. Microwave the broccoli according to the package directions. (Plot them on a microwave-safe plate and sprinkle with a few tablespoons of water if you're using fresh broccoli). *Cover with plastic wrap and microwave 3-5 minutes or until crisp-tender.*
3. Remove and sprinkle with the Lemon Crumbs and olive oil.

Hearty Red Bell Pepper and Green Bean Toss

A very hearty and delicious way to sneak more vegetables into your diet. This veggie medley goes fantastic with chicken, eggs, fish, and especially steak. This recipe does not use the grill, unless you have cooked vegetables stashed in the fridge ready to go.

Ingredients:

- 2 tablespoons butter
- 2 (8-oz.) packages French green beans
- 1 red bell pepper, cut into thin strips
- 3 shallots, sliced
- 2 garlic cloves, minced
- 1/2 teaspoon salt
- 1/8 teaspoon ground red pepper

Directions:

1. Melt some butter in a skillet and throw in the green beans, bell pepper strips, and remaining ingredients, tossing to evenly coat.
2. Add 1/4 cup water.
3. Cook the vegetables for 4-6 minutes with a lid.
4. Remove the lid and cook, stirring often, 1-2 more minutes or until water is mostly evaporated and the beans are tender.

Creamed Corn

Who doesn't love creamed corn? It's the perfect side dish to serve up with any meal. Very simple and easy to make -- a favorite among kids and adults alike. This dish does not use the grill to prepare, apart from the bacon.

Ingredients:

- 1/4 cup butter or margarine
- 2 1/2 cups fresh corn kernels (about 8 ears)
- 1/2 cup milk
- 1 tablespoon cornstarch
- 1 tablespoon sugar
- 1/2 teaspoon salt

Directions:

1. Grab a large skillet and spoon some butter over medium heat.
2. Stir in the corn kernels and milk.
3. Now sprinkle in the cornstarch, sugar, and salt -- stir well *(this is important!)*.
4. Bring the entire mixture to a boil, stirring constantly.
5. Reduce heat to a simmer, STILL stirring constantly, for about 10-12 minutes. Serve hot and fresh for best taste.

To serve with bacon and leeks:
1. Preheat the grill to medium-high heat.
2. Add the bacon strips until they're crispy *(or to your liking)*
3. Remove the bacon and chop them into strips.
4. Chop some leeks as well and sprinkle both over the finished dish.

Honey-Glazed Carrot Circles

This dish does not use the grill to prepare. It pairs well with any of the meat recipes in this book because it is straight-up healthy and delicious. It's a perfect side dish to prepare while the chicken or beef is cooking.

Ingredients:

- 1 1/2 quarts water
- 5 cups thinly sliced carrots
- 3 tablespoons chopped fresh parsley
- 2 tablespoons honey
- 1/2 teaspoon salt
- 1/2 teaspoon grated orange rind
- 1/4 teaspoon freshly ground black pepper

Directions:

1. Boil a pot of water in a medium-sized saucepan.
2. Throw in the carrots and cook for 20 min, or until they're tender.
3. Drain the water and mix the carrots and remaining ingredients in a large bow. Mix well.

Perfectly Roasted Sweet Potato Wedges

Finally, who doesn't love fried potatoes? They pretty much go great with just about anything, even by themselves! The best part is that this one is a healthy alternative to the oily fast food ones. Have the potatoes chopped and seasoned to throw them in the grill with your favorite meat for the perfect side.

Ingredients:

- 2 tablespoons olive oil
- 3 tablespoons brown sugar
- 1/4 teaspoon ground nutmeg
- Kosher salt and pepper
- 4 pounds small sweet potatoes, each peeled and cut into 8 wedges
- 8 sprigs thyme

Directions:

1. Combine the following ingredients in a large bowl: oil, sugar, nutmeg, 1 teaspoon salt, and 1/2 teaspoon pepper.
2. Throw in the sweet potato wedges and shake vigorously to coat evenly.
3. Preheat the grill to medium-high heat.
4. Place the wedges on the grill and let them cook until they start browning.
5. Flip after about 5-6 min, or until the edges are dark brown and the wedges are crisp.

Made in the USA
Lexington, KY
13 February 2015